YOU AND I NEED WATER TO SURVIVE!

CHEMISTRY BOOK FOR BEGINNERS
Children's Chemistry Books

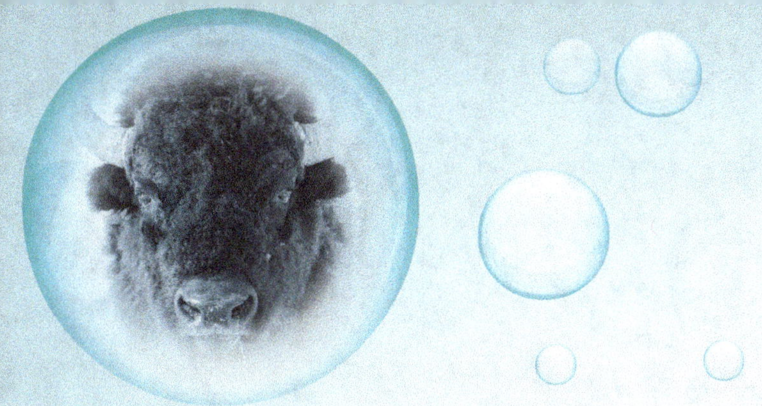

Buffalo

Rose

If you're a bug or a buffalo or a blossoming rose bush, you need water to survive. Without water, life as we know it on Earth would not be possible. Read on and find out more about this wonderful liquid!

Ladybug

WHERE DOES WATER COME FROM?

Water is a combination of two elements, hydrogen and oxygen. Two hydrogen atoms combine with one oxygen atom to make water, and scientists write that as H_2O.

But where do hydrogen and oxygen come from?

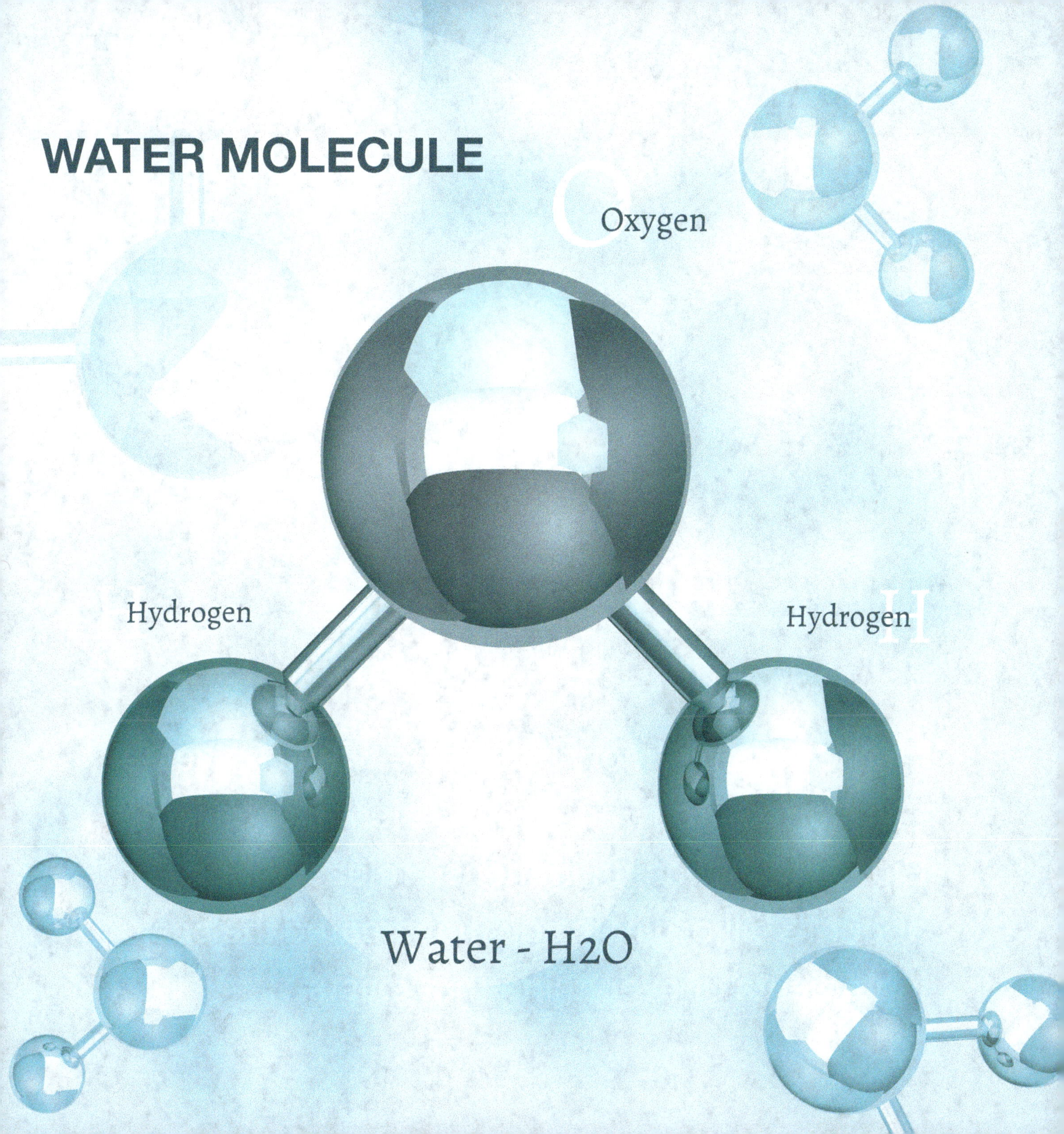

WATER MOLECULE
Oxygen
Hydrogen
Hydrogen
Water - H2O

THE BIG BANG

The current theory is that the whole universe started from an event scientists call the Big Bang. It was an immense release of power about 13 billion years ago that created the basic ingredients of everything that exists

BIG BANG THEORY
METRIC EXPANSION OF SPACE

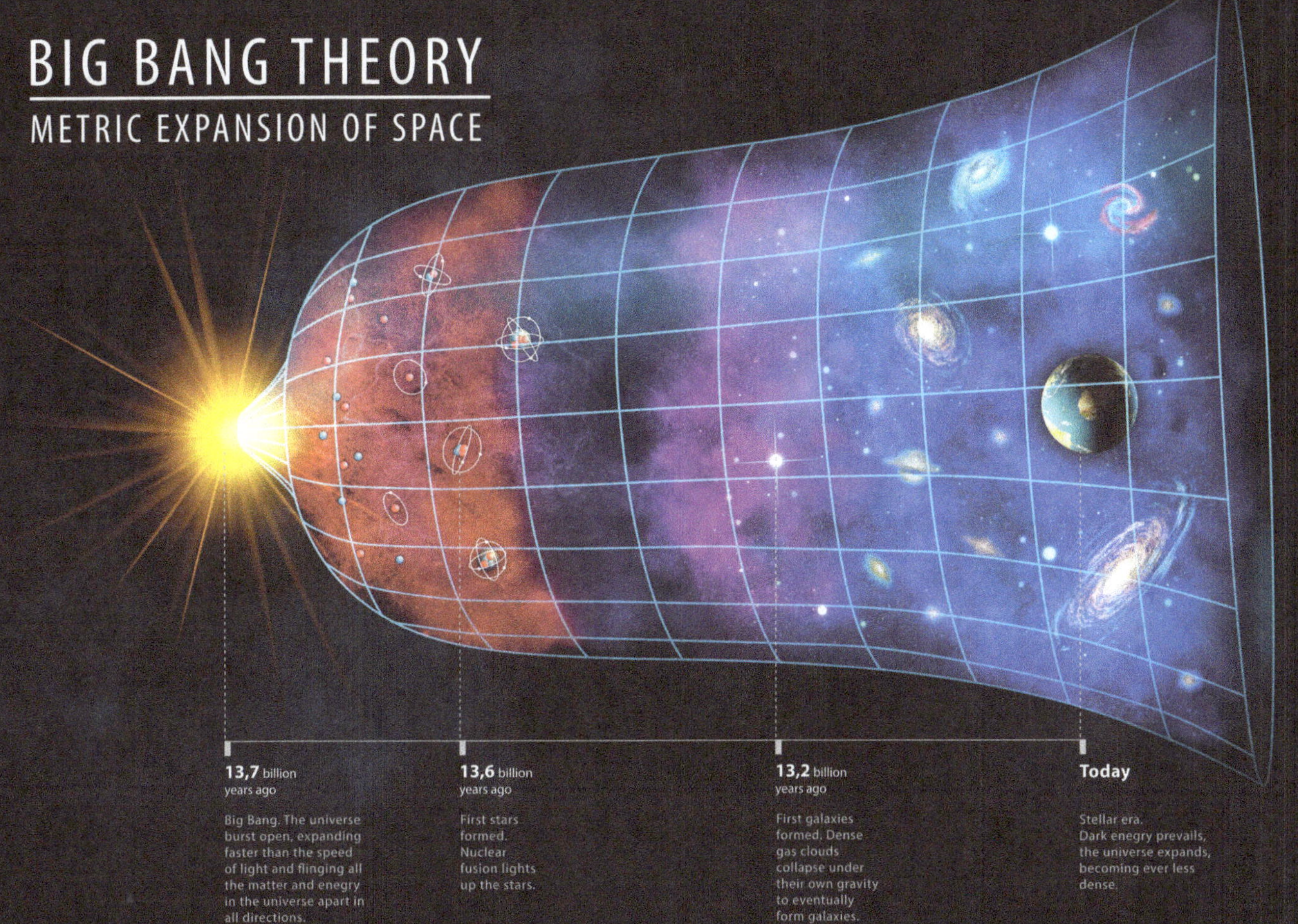

Within the first few minutes of the Big Bang, the primal material crashed and smashed together, and created the simplest elements: hydrogen, helium and lithium. So now we have the H_2 part.

In fact, H_2, hydrogen gas, is the most common molecule in the universe.

MAKING OXYGEN

Scientists think that millions or billions of years had to pass before oxygen became available. Stars created oxygen, carbon, and the other more complex elements in their incredibly-hot and high-pressure centers. Then when a star dies (explodes as a super-nova) it releases all those elements into the universe. Stars the size of our Sun create the oxygen needed for 100 million Amazon Rivers every second.

Now we have a lot of O floating around.

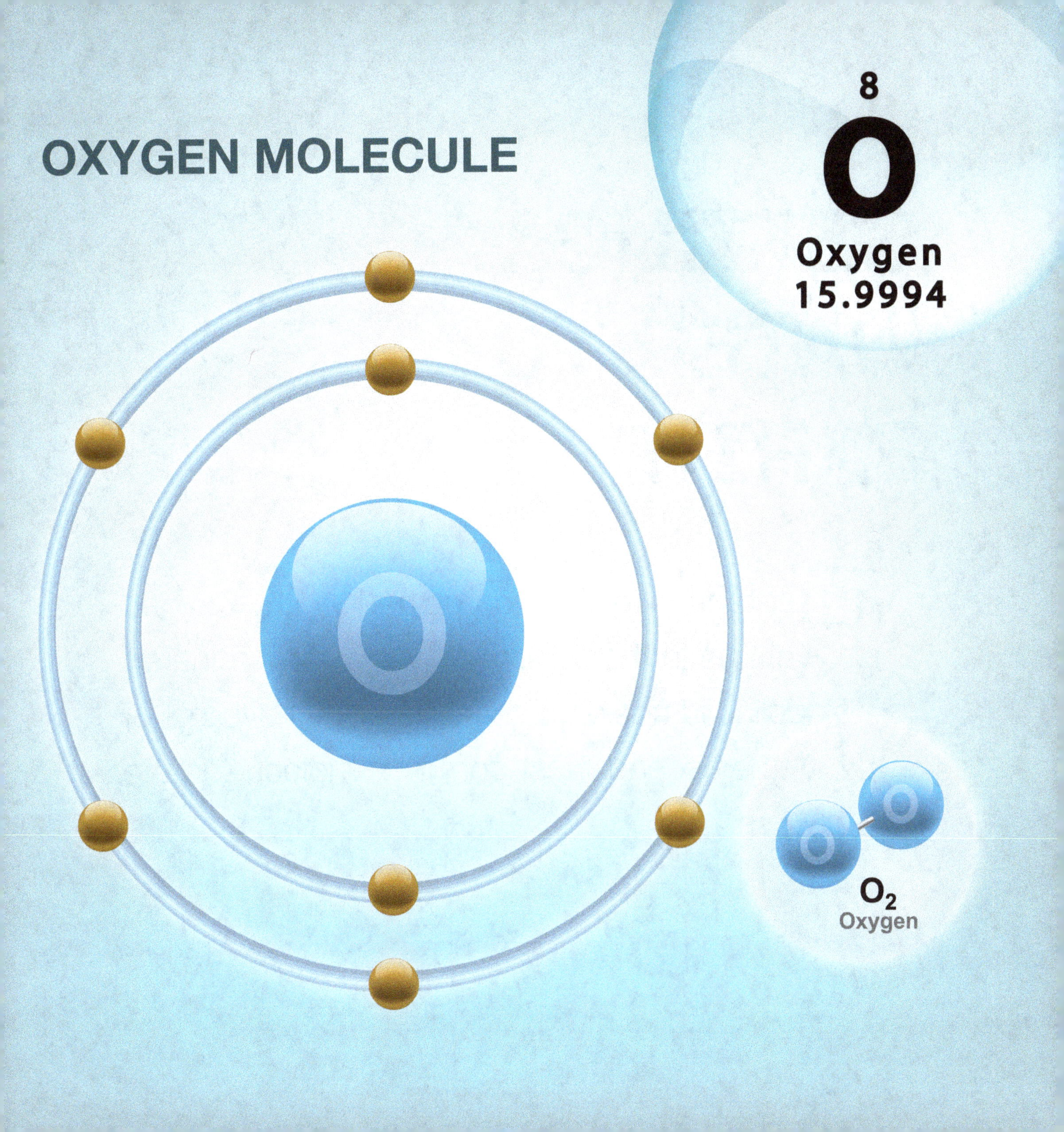

OXYGEN MOLECULE

8

O

Oxygen
15.9994

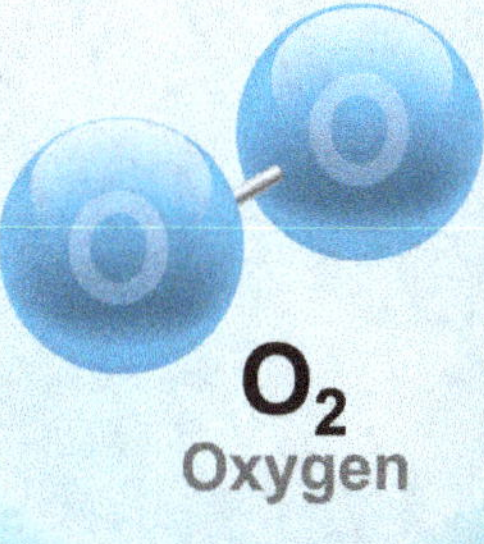

GETTING WATER TO EARTH

Hydrogen atoms combined with oxygen atoms in the cooling universe, and adhered to cooling lumps of material. Now we have lots of H_2O, the second most common molecule in the universe.

WATER STRUCTURE FORMATION

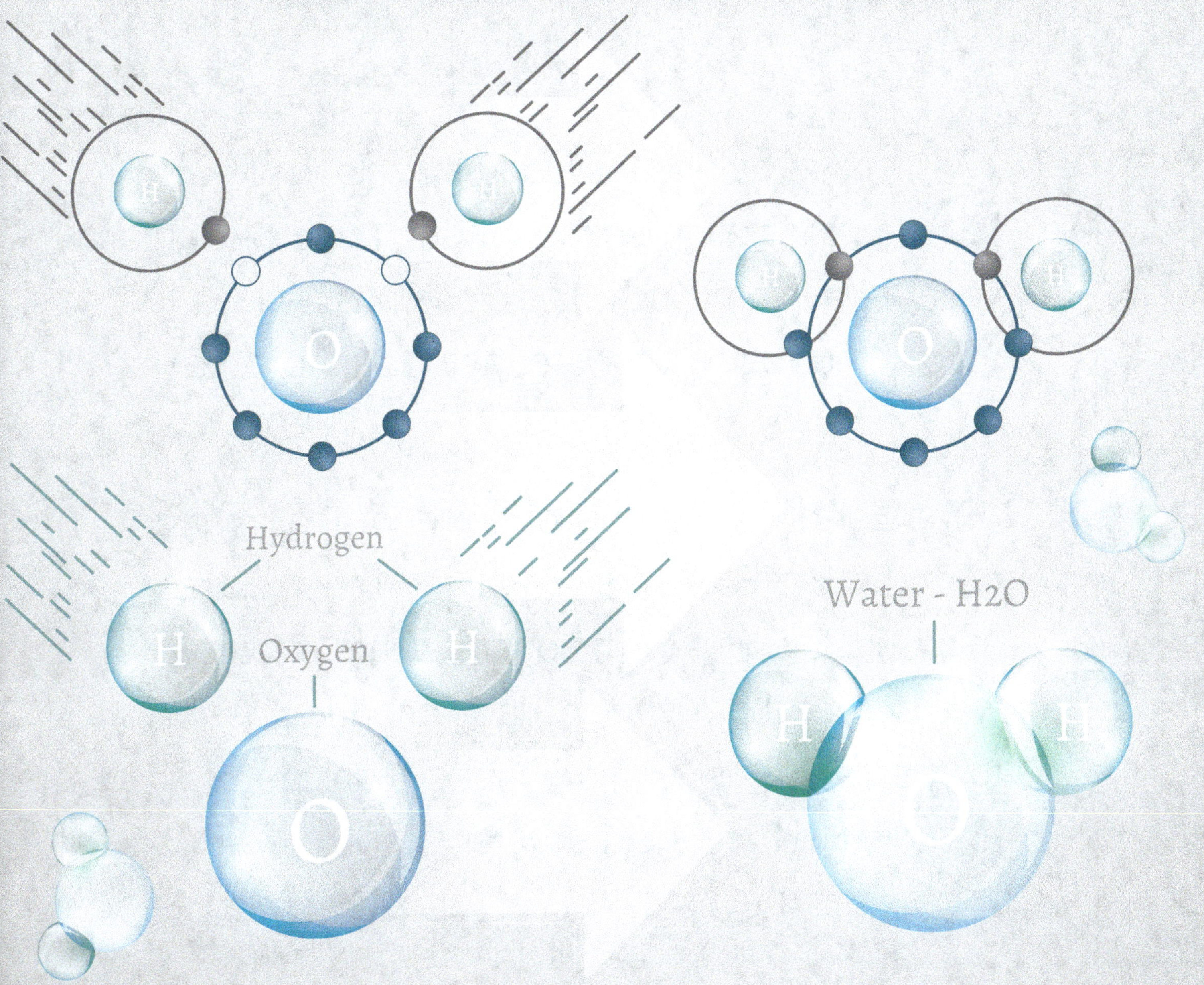

Scientists have identified a huge cloud of water vapor far off in space, about 12 billion light years away from Earth. The cloud has about 140 trillion times as much water as do all the oceans on Earth.

The Earth is made up of some of that matter from the Big Bang, as are all the other planets and our Sun. But for billions of years, the Earth was so hot that it would have been impossible for water to exist on its surface or inside it. So how did the Earth get its water?

Universe starscape backdrop with space clouds

Comet in the starry sky

A lot of other, smaller lumps of matter cooled down so they could host frozen water much sooner than Earth did. These smaller lumps are asteroids, comets, proto-planets and general space debris.

As the Earth cooled, and all through its early history, it was bombarded by other pieces of material traveling through space after the Big Bang. Comets brushed past the earth, asteroids collided with it. Each visitor dropped off some of its material-iron, carbon, other materials and, once the Earth was cool enough to receive it, H_2O. Pretty much all the water we have on the Earth was delivered to us by other objects traveling through space!

Earth, Galaxy and Sun

THE WATER CYCLE

The water that we have now is the same amount the Earth had in the time of the dinosaurs. Water spends time in the rivers and oceans. The oceans cover about 70% of the surface of the Earth.

Highly detailed planet Earth in the morning

Water cycle diagram

The surface of bodies of water evaporate and become water vapor in the air. Water vapor collects into water droplets in clouds and eventually rains back down on the water and on dry land. And all the water eventually finds its way down to the oceans again.

Over the course of a hundred years, a water molecule will spend about 98 years in the ocean, less than a year as ice, about two weeks in freshwater rivers and lakes, and about a week as vapor in the air.

Water molecule structure

Migration animals drinking water

On the way through this cycle, water can spend time as parts of plants and animals. It nourishes living creatures and, when they don't need it any more, the water passes out of them and continues its journey through its cycle.

STATES OF WATER

ater can exist in three different states on this planet. Between 0 and 100 degrees Celsius at sea level, water is a liquid. When it gets colder than 0 degrees Celsius, it takes a solid form: ice. When it gets hotter than 100 degrees Celsius, it turns into a vapor. The temperature range is a little different if you are high up on a mountain, where the air pressure is less.

WATER STATES

The Moon and the planet Earth

Although water exists as ice on other planets, and on the moons of some planets, in our universe, Earth is the only place we know of so far where all three states of water can exist.

STICKY WATER

Another special thing about water is that its molecules stick tightly to each other, and to other objects. If you look closely at the water in a drinking glass, the edges of the very top of the water rise up a little bit along the inside of the glass. This is "surface tension" holding the water together.

   If water were not so sticky it would be a gas at room temperature, the way similar molecules like ammonia (a nitrogen atom and three hydrogen atoms, or NH_3) are. And if water were a gas at room temperature, we would not exist.

Bottled water poured in glass

WATER AND THE WORLD

Here are some interesting facts about water on our watery planet, the Earth:

WHERE THE WATER IS

Almost 97% of all water is in the salty oceans or deep underground. About 2% is frozen into glaciers and the ice at the North and South Poles. That means that all plants and all animals, including you and me, share just 1% of the world's water.

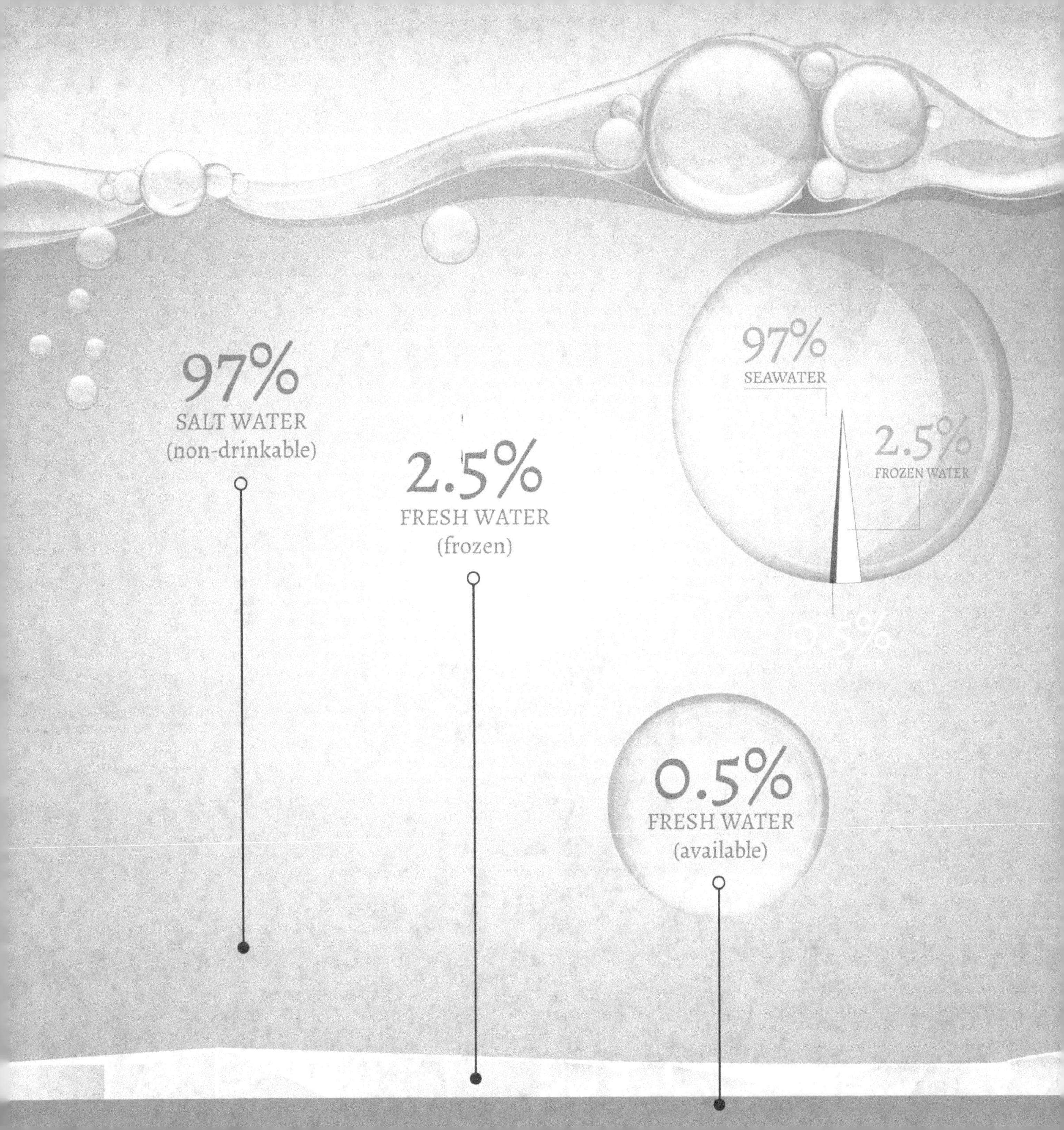

97%
SALT WATER
(non-drinkable)

2.5%
FRESH WATER
(frozen)

0.5%
FRESH WATER
(available)

97%
SEAWATER

2.5%
FROZEN WATER

0.5%

Man pours boiling water demonstrating frost effect as hot water freezes quickly

THE MPEMBA EFFECT

Hot water freezes more quickly than cold water. We know this happens, but we don't know why.

WHY ICE FLOATS

When water freezes, it expands. The same amount of water is about 9% larger in volume when it is ice. Since the same material is filling a larger volume, it is lighter as ice than when it is liquid. This is why ice floats on water.

Ices and icebergs of unusual forms and colors.

PURE WATER
Pure water has no smell and no taste.

water background

Bottled water

CARRYING WATER

Water weighs about eight pounds a gallon. In its liquid state, water does not compress.

WATER AND PEOPLE

We would be nothing without water. Here are some things to know about water and your body:

A WET BODY

The adult human body is almost 70% water. As a baby develops in the womb, it starts at around 90% water. When the baby is born, it is about 78% water.

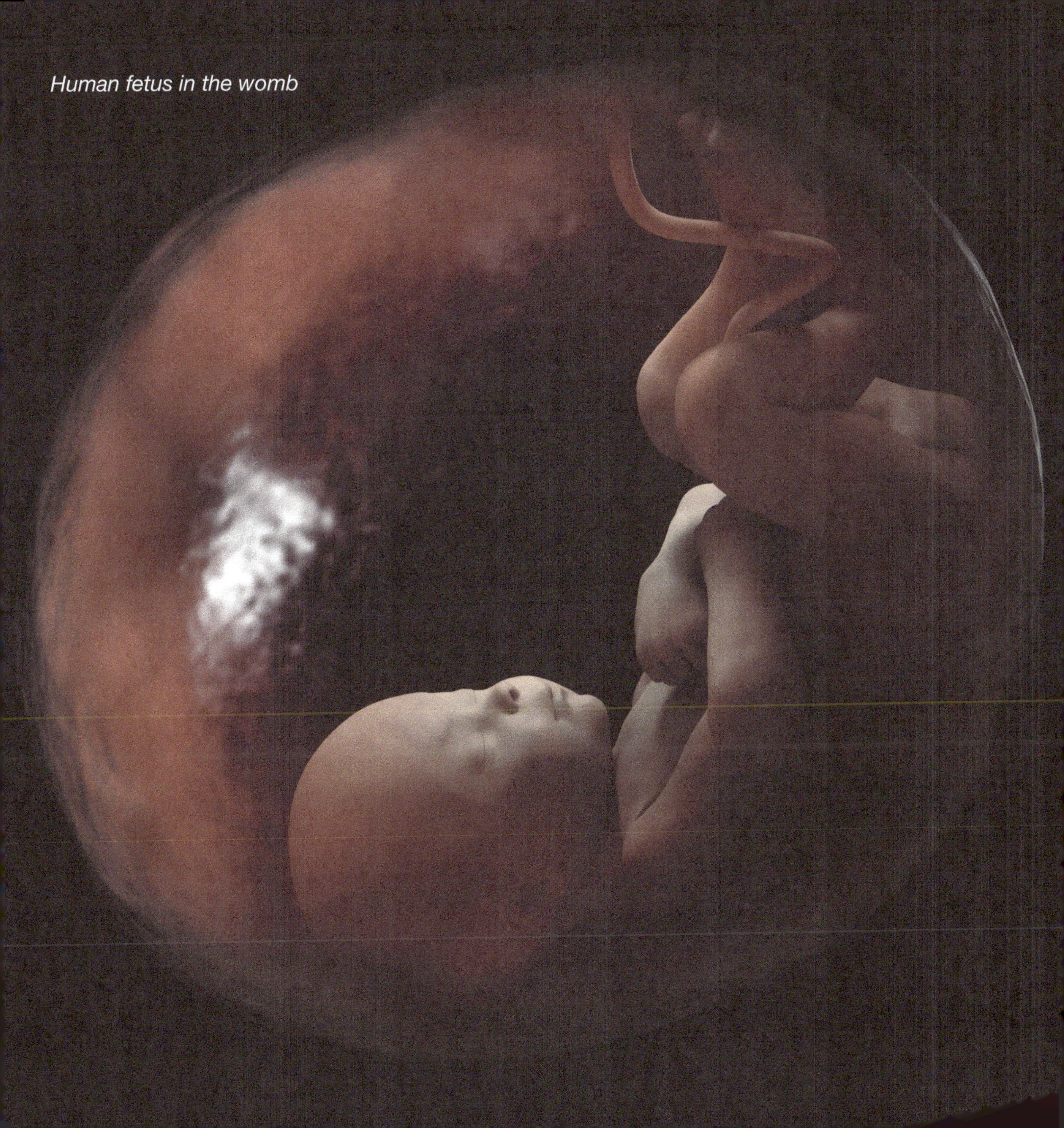
Human fetus in the womb

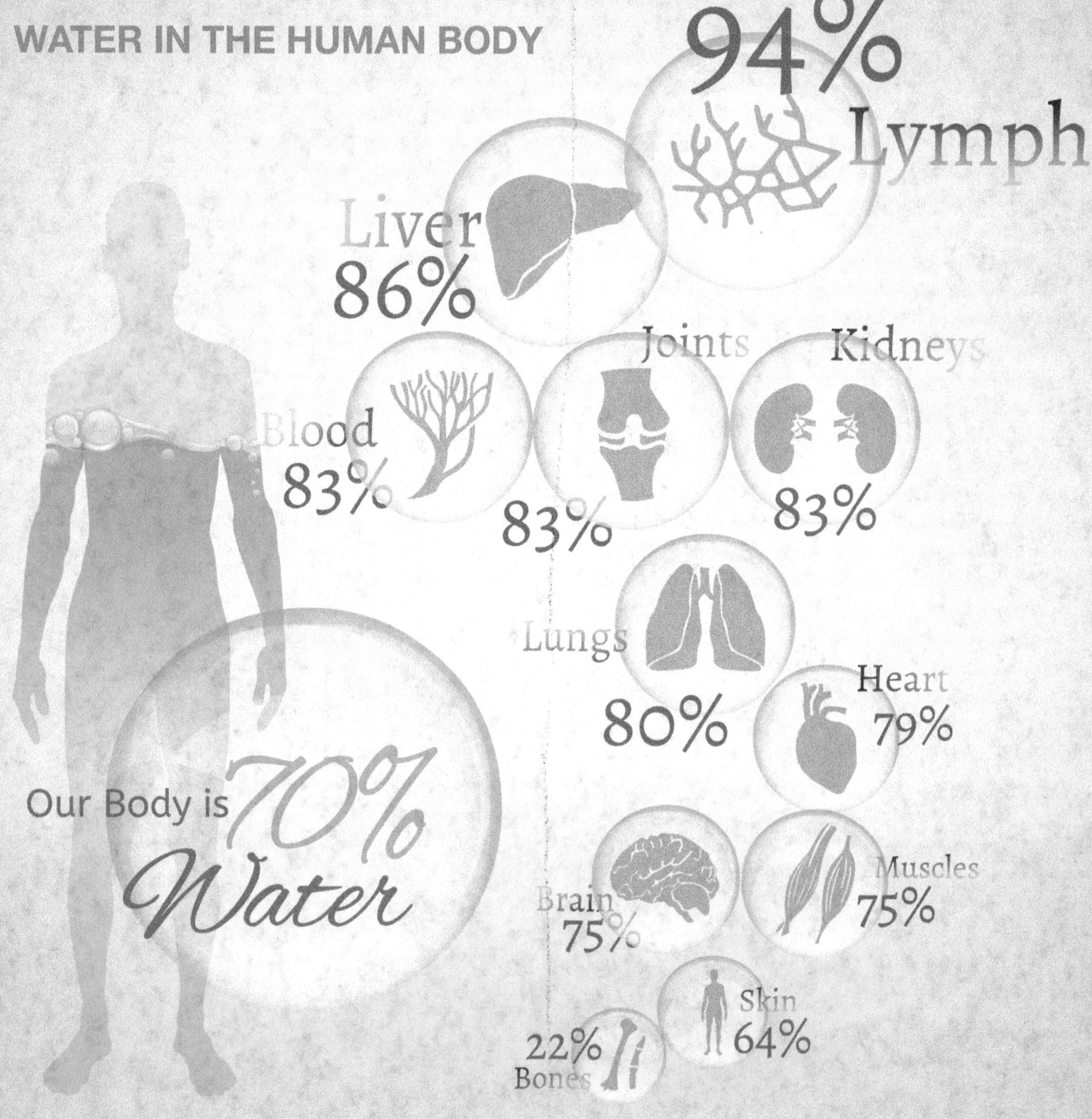

WATER IN THE HUMAN BODY
94%
Lymph
Liver
86%
Joints
Kidneys
Blood
83%
83%
83%
Lungs
Heart
79%
80%
Our Body is 70% Water
Brain
75%
Muscles
75%
Skin
64%
22%
Bones

Two thirds of the water in your body is in your cells. More is in your blood stream and helps make up the lining of your digestive system as well as the lining of your lungs.

WATER ON THE BRAIN

About 75% of your brain is made up of water.

Brain
75%

Our Body is 70%
Water

Newborn baby sleeping in blanket

BABIES AND WATER

Pound for pound, babies need seven times as much water each day as adults do.

HUNGER AND THIRST

If you really had to, you could live up to a month without food. But you could only live maybe a week without water.

Little girl drinking water

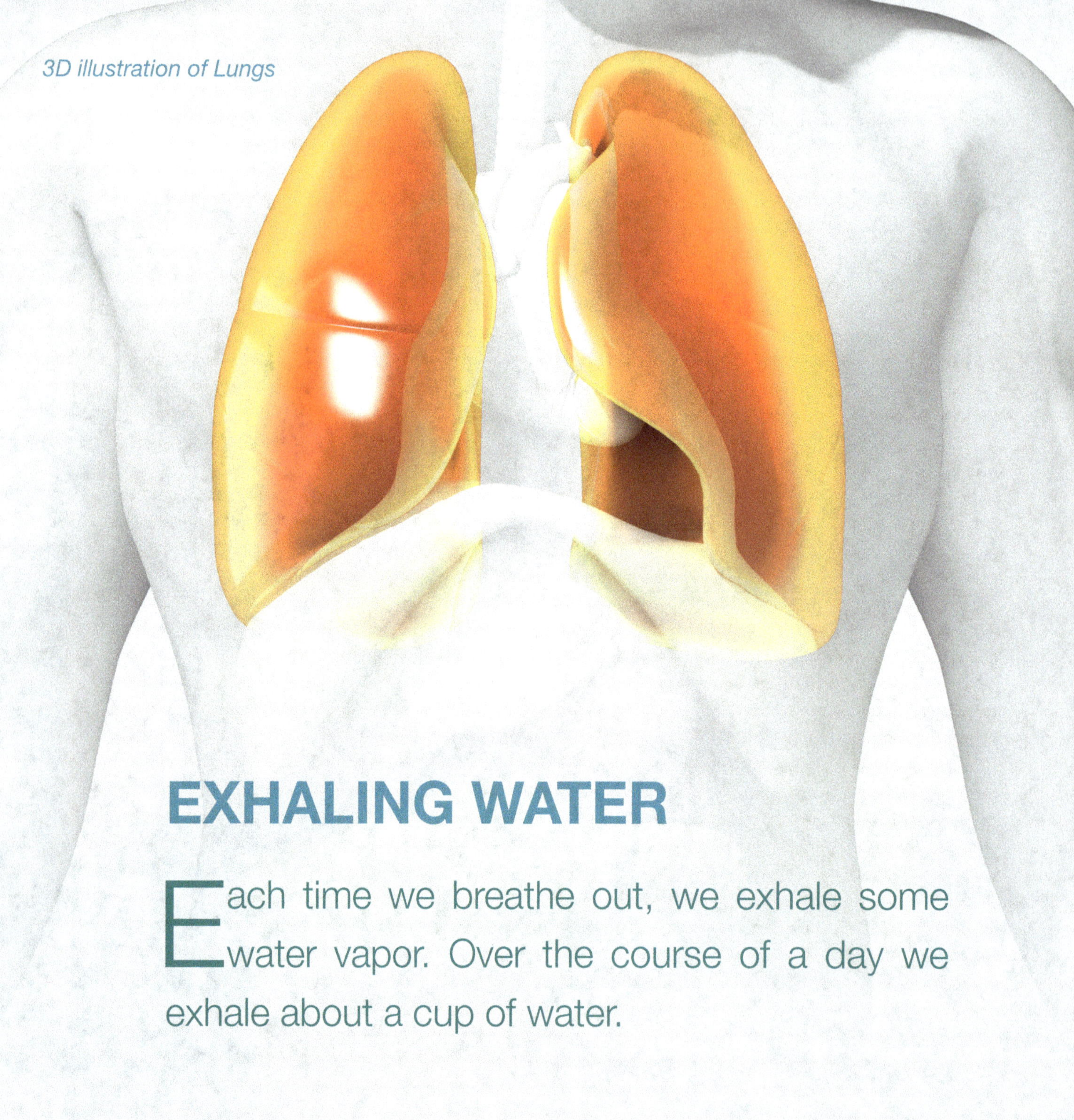

EXHALING WATER

Each time we breathe out, we exhale some water vapor. Over the course of a day we exhale about a cup of water.

DAILY RATION

Taking into account all uses of water, including washing, drinking, flushing toilets and producing food (watering crops and giving water to animals), each person requires about 12 gallons of water a day.

SAFE WATER

Alot of people buy and drink bottled water. Hundreds of millions of people around the world do not have access to clean, safe water. About 80% all the illnesses in poorer countries, the "developing world", is connected to the lack of clean, safe water.

One third of what everyone on Earth spends for bottled water would pay for providing fresh water to everybody who does not now have it.

Indian woman drawing water from the well

WATER USE

Each year in North America, the average house-hold uses over 100,000 gallons of water for everything from cooking to flushing the toilet to watering the lawn.

A RESOURCE TO FIGHT OVER

We know of at least 200 wars that different nations or tribes have fought with other peoples over access to water since about 3,000 BCE.

WATER PRESSURE

Over the last hundred years the rate of water use per person has increased at twice the rate of population growth. There are many more of us, and we are using a lot more water than people used to!

SAVING WATER

If every household in the United States flushes the toilet once, that uses enough fresh water to fill a lake a mile long, a mile wide, and four feet deep. A little less flushing would save a lot of water!

WASTING WATER

If you have a tap in your house that drips a little water all the time, maybe one drip each second, that tap is wasting over 3,000 gallons of fresh water each year.

LEARN MORE ABOUT YOUR BODY AND YOUR WORLD

There is always more to learn! Our planet and our bodies keep showing us surprises. Read other Baby Professor books, like *Peeling the Earth Like an Onion* and *Top 50 Quick Facts about the Human Body*, to learn more!

Visit

BABY PROFESSOR
EDUCATION KIDS

www.BabyProfessorBooks.com

to download Free Baby Professor eBooks and view
our catalog of new and exciting Children's Books